Ride The World
Poems

By
Stephen R. Dilley IV
and
Esteban V. Irigoyen

Ride The World Poems

By
Stephen R. Dilley IV
and
Esteban U. Irigoyen

E-BookTime, LLC
Montgomery, Alabama

Ride The World Poems

Library of Congress Control Number: 2013940555

ISBN: 978-1-60862-495-9

First Edition
Published December 2014
E-BookTime, LLC
6598 Pumpkin Road
Montgomery, AL 36108
www.e-booktime.com

Contents

Contents

Beauty Lies in the Heart and Soul

Beauty lies in the heart and soul,
As tender as a feather and malleable as gold,
Beauty lies beneath the eyes,
Where omniscient colors and shiny hair lie,
So look not with an ugly eye,
Beauty comes in every shape and size,
So make a judgment and make it wise.

Man's Whimsical Dream

What do men dream of? It is glowing stars, majestic skies, and
soaring horizons which make man's
eyes twinkle in grandeur. He finds
bliss in being loved, and his heart beats on. He finds hope in
the words of older, wiser men who treasure freedom and liberty.
He dreams of triumphs and he perseveres
through cold, dark nights in search of that whimsical
dream. His ideas span the sparkling oceans and are carried
over tides across the world from sea to shore,
from spacious mountains and valleys as
he dreams of sacred forests with gardens and waterfalls
from which life ebbs and flows.
As he dreams of blissful parks and sunlit pastures and
quiet nights with overhead stars that reflect light,
giving warmth to splendorous grassy lands in
regal countryside's. He dreams all this as he ponders
his reflection, painted over the
surface of a clear pond, in a peaceful heather grove
of his sublime dream world.

Noah's Boat

In the far distance out at sea
on his back lay an old man in his boat,
admiring the soaring flight of the seagulls through the
crystal blue skies
in his tranquil blue maritime world.
He dreamed of unknown worlds that lay ahead
and hot dry cocoa beaches extending along every shore
with sea life of every color
to capture an experienced captain's eyes.
As the sun set and darkness covered the skies
the thundering waves began to heave the boat.
Noah, the intrepid sailor, grasped the wheel
and terrified of the Almighty's wrath,
exclaimed: "For what have I done my God? Spare me.
I worship only thee
and try to live as virtuously as possible.
I neither hate nor disobey.
I'm not sinful as others may have been.
I'm righteous and obedient,
and most importantly, I love.
The lands of the avaricious, selfish, greedy, and sinful
who break your laws,
I have abandoned."
But before he could grasp the sail,
the seas crashed and the thunderous lightning flashed.
He awoke in his boat three days later,
in the heart of a fertile
green pasture, in the land of plentiful,
surrounded by creatures of every stripe and flock,
and flowers of every color.

Wolves

Through the cold night, I wandered in the forest
gazing at the full moon that hung like an ornament.
Then I remembered it was the night of Halloween when
creatures search for blood in the midnight dreary hour. I cried,
"Help thou! Does anybody hear me?" But nobody was there.
In the stillness of the night, howling grizzly wolves
crept around me.
"Be gone satanic spawn!" I cried.
But no one was there for me.
Reaching in my pocket lay a gun.
Should I kill myself and end my misery?
Suicide crossed my mind, but I don't want to go to hell.
What other option have I? I stood horrified.
Everyone who cared for me has left.
But then I remembered my days as a criminal when I did
so many wrongs and little good.
God decreed eternal punishment for the sinner.
"Eat me devils. Nothing better than to die on my judgment day!"
As wolves chewed ferociously consuming my flesh on
my last day on earth.

Fallen

Placed in the dark underworld,
those previously angelical beings,
half-man, half-woman,
were cast away to a lake of brimstone and fire
to burn with other fallen souls.
Their flesh was being torn apart by
the flaming winds of the dark underworld
as their monstrous bodies transformed into
part minotaur part snake, becoming ever so hideous.
There were gargoyles in flight like bats,
but breathing breaths of fire
in that netherworld.
Therein lived skeletons of grim reapers,
swinging their scythes away
at the flesh of the dead as hounds of hell
raised a raucous, howling, mournful
sound as the bodies cindered.
Therein serpents hissed as the fallen ones
grew horns on their head and rat tails between their legs.
They had become demons roaming about the
nebulous endless sky prison.
They were condemned to tempting humans on earth to sin.
Their purpose
was to grow armies at all four corners of the world,
and to prey on the countless weak minds.
Forever, these demons
would be feasting on the fallen souls,
whose integer power grew logarithmically with base six,
while the ravenous demons' numbers increased exponentially
with irrational exponents.

The wasteland was a chaotic ensemble
of doomed castaways from the promised lands
whose cursed lies would consume
them in their elliptical prison pit.

Dogcat

Oh that wretched cat thought I,
again creeping gracefully along my fence,
as its feline green eyes preyed on me.
Oh that devious cat,
is to me like an insect crawling in the shadows along
the crevices of the floor.
That crafty, duplicitous cat
has eluded me for years.
"But what would become
of it, were I to call the animal shelter?" I thought.
Surely it will be out of its misery.
No more nine lives for him!
It has survived all of these feline
years while I have stood here all these
human years doing nothing.
I knuckle my fist to my mouth. For years,
it has pounced on my pet mice and
chased away my beautiful, peaceful squirrels
whom I love to see nestled in my trees
this time of year. Surely I will strangle that darn dark cat.
Should I shoot it with my pellet gun?
If it eludes me once again,
do I simply surrender to its will for survival
and its craftiness?

Perhaps of natural causes it will soon die,
thus exonerating me of ill will towards an animal.
Indeed, I am now smiling and happier for this purer thought.

Until the dreadful day arrived, I wept.
The old cat had come back to haunt me by
stirring up memories of a special friend.
It had a bone in its mouth
and it meowed before me. It fancied my company
as did I. I shed a few more tears.
It greeted me with a meow and frozen – it stared straight at me.
This time in the glint and reflection of its greenish eyes, I
knew I was staring at the soul of my
faithful and beloved dog who decades ago, had passed away.
A wave of emotions was triggered
by this sublime memory of my best friend.
Happiness engulfed me. I saw my dog
in the cat's pupil and for many years
since, I have adored and cherished that feline
in my arms. My beloved
dog now lives in the spirit of the cat, so be fooled not
by the change in growl. Beloved creatures each, or
both, or one and the same. A surreal attachment
surrounds us, and only this creature and I know
the truth. My friend has returned at last.

The Saved Doll

Her soothing marble eyes were like those of
the antique doll she remembered having cuddled as a child.
No longer in her mother's womb,
she now lay in her mother's arms
staring up at those gentle expressive eyes and the soft curvature
of her cheeks – her mother's gift to her.
Her mother, startled by the sound of a baby's shrill,
prayed the rosary of the Virgin Mary on the altar.
Meanwhile, envious, devilish gargoyles
fiendishly ranted damnation,
while the nervous mother–
fearing the demonically, stoic and possessive powers
being thrust into
her holy mind from the claws of a callused devil–
prayed feverishly.
The luster surface of her rigid face reflected the
denial of any wicked
thoughts, since it had been cleansed by holy water
and thus freed from curse.
Heaven's gates swung open and her craftsman maker
embraced his
very own divine creation: the saved doll's soul.

Exquisite Fellow

Looking fresh with slicked back black hair,
and armed with gold-rimmed sunglasses
he strolls the streets with his charming
megawatt smile, looking for another Barbie girl.
One date after another,
bras become unhinged, and panties fall.
There's smothered kisses on his face,
and lipstick smeared on fine silk dress shirts.
Wrapped in a fancy grey trench coat, his well-toned muscles
and fine adoring face soothe
countless women's capricious hearts.
The envy of his male friends,
and the ideal partner of fond female friends he is.

Pit

In the pit lie a place for the cunning
who deceive humankind where
I watched bitter, unrepentant people burn.
I questioned my life.
Had I lived righteously?
I admit to a sinner's life.
Had I lived in virtue?
But I helped the needy, I
cried as I struggled to break free
from the torment. In the hollow I lived in damnation,
shedding tears for thee.
In the depths below dwelled horrific,
monsters, and goblins who lurked in the crevices
where demons sucked the blood
of bewildered humans who
committed unrighteous, immoral deeds.
Where is St. Peter, the man who opens
heaven's gates?
I wept again looking through
the dimness of what little light, there was.
Trying to break free of the hellish hole,
I was left in darkness.
Then I saw a hand, as a fallen hellion
tugged at my leg, leeching and pulling me
down to the furnace below.
Seeing the heavens father outstretched hand grasp my arm,
I clinched it, as a voice said to me "Choose the path my son:
A life of misery where evil-doers live,
or a place of peace, your heavenly father makes for thee."

I opened my eyes to see the morning light,
and yawned as I heard the chirps of birds,
and the firmament above
turned faint and lazy.
It was but a dream.
Hence, I must do good, for in the pit of despair lie the damned.

Venomous

The venomous serpent lay
in the glistening mouth of the reptilian
woman, as the snake vented
and slithered in her mouth.
She was becoming
even more snake-like and insidious.
Then, the transformation began.
In the eyes of the condemned, she became
a deity. She was ever
so demonic, yet a creation of
the Gods, to serve as the queen of
the reptiles, like the Naga
and the dinosaurs that
roamed earth years ago.

Heaven Bound

Although a crazed fool they've thought me to be,
all through the night towards sky I gazed at thee.
Then I remembered to check if in the heavens you did lie,
I reached to touch the many billions of stars,
but only found myself heaven bound.
Like a bird, I felt lifted, as if destined to another place–
transported through Stargate to await my fate.
Where am I going I did ask?
Have I died and left mind, body and soul behind?
Has my deathbed arrived so soon on this full moon lit night?
Among this firmament, this celestial beauty his testament,
where's God, the king of stars?
Then I remembered how good and pious I had been,
for need not worry I should be,
because in passing to this kingdom,
among spirits and angels I'd soon be.

Gift

There I stood staring through the window,
looking through the glass at the box.
I had visions of goods and toys which I fantasized.
What might it be?
My imagination jumped from dreams of
elaborate game boards, to video game thrills,
to books that fascinate a bookworm scholar.
I can only ponder what I will do with this gift
that dazzles my senses.
As I peek at the sleet
covered by snow, I see a red ribbon tied to it.
I wonder whether or not to open the gift.
A temptation for the curious.
It's there but for who? A present from whom?
I watched as the
snowflakes sparkled, emitting their red brilliance, wrapped
in velveteen – almost perfect – so precious.
If I never take it, then I shall always wonder
the mystery of the gift that lay inside will forever
be a secret.

Ariel

There it was clear and buoyant, the opaque ocean
carrying its waves beautifully, eventfully,
with sea creatures bathing in the sand as seagulls
soared in the sky. The full moon showcased
during the midnight hour, when the stars twinkled and
the sea faded as the tides reached the
shore. Then in the clearness, I had a tranquil vision
in which mermaids splashed and wacked their tails
in the sand. I walked into the shallow water
and took a dive in the marine,
to be with Ariel,
whose cremated ashes lay sprinkled in the deep,
after being laid to rest years ago.
Now I could see my darling girl living in
peace with a glossy pearl beside her in a huge open
clam. Our love was eternal. Then slowly it closed.
I was to be with her for eternity.

Greed

A cold, low, heart have I,
so stingy I can be,
for I care only for myself.
With only money and self-pride on my mind,
my greed is fed with big checks and
fancy credit cards I
use for personal pleasure.
Oh I'm Mr. Greed. Little
is spent on my wife as I
use her only for lustful sex.
As for the little children? Only five dollars
for each birthday and socks and underwear
at Christmas time. Ha! I laugh! Those little brats.
I'm scrooge, they say
I spend it all on grown up toys, like fine automobiles,
penthouses and expensive ladies
to soothe my ego.
All of this for me and no one else. For the
banks feed me millions of dollars each week in interest
while others beg on the streets.
Needy they may be, but I say 'No!'.
Depriving families, friends, and co-workers – so sordid I be,
for riches mean everything for the greedy me.

Garage

In the garage lay saws to cut away,
shovels to plant flowers, and luminous trees,
dolls for little girls to play with,
paints to paint away,
ladders to climb to the sky, old video
game machines for the gamer, duster
blowers for the dirty back yard, weed whackers
for the weeds which seemingly could touch the sky.
Old shoes withering away, waiting for a shoe
repair, pictures and art for a festival,
hammers and tools for a blacksmith,
garbage bags for the unkempt house,
books for bookworms and scholars,
a place where automobiles can rest,
a pleasant place
that brings feelings of unbridled imagination,
where one could spend an entire year just
looking at one's junk and other personal memorabilia.
A place in time where you could feel nostalgic and
saddened with tears
for a passing grandfather that you smiled
at in your adolescent years,
remembering all those years
you spent together hugging, and loving, each other
as those golden years went by.

Memory

Like a sound of thunder the snow poured down,
and the hail crackled as
my face turned
white, happy like an angel.
I saw a frosty snowman with blushing red
cheeks – my heart frozen
through time. My eyes were as
clear as white sleet,
as I dashed down the mountain
in a sled made of gold. There
with my brother, as cold as
ice and with a passion hungry
for winter. Two hearts
bound by love – irresistible –
a slush world in a
cold forest land.
As reindeer followed,
dancing through the frozen
flakes, I saw Santa.

Honey

Honey, oh honey, your queen
hiding in a bee's hive,
so deliciously sweet
the nectar of life.
Yummy to fill my tummy,
from a honeybee's hive.
Oh my darling queen bee
whom I adore,
one great hun full of love.
Oh my lover bee,
be with me these
days turned to loving,
the honeysuckle
that you suck of
and that I eat of you,
my darling beloved honey bun.

Forest

Its tall green alluring grass,
beauteous riverbeds, and rolling mountains
which breath cool misty clouds, all captivate the naked eye.
Its jovial animals bring pride to its myriad species,
like the lonesome wolf,
thirsty and scavenging to appease its hunger.
And the roaring bear, king of the forest, only wants his honey.
Then there's the doe who nestles in her den,
while the reindeer
mince grass peacefully. But suddenly they flee, hearing the
sounds of gunshots as hunters gather in numbers, killing
the fawn who prances gleefully.
Sad are the deer, for the
pyromaniac men have no
fondness for peace, but burn the forest to ashes.
Tearful is mother nature, sobbing as its rainy tears
seep the warm roots of every tree and flower.
The lustrous
woods where campers gather,
await to showcase mother nature's
outdoors.

Rich

Feeling that touch of love that never
leaves from the labor that makes,
us strive so we serve our country,
seeking fame and fortune,
rich we become.
To beloved spouses we marry,
at a wedding,
soon having sex,
as man and woman
romance, as male injects
his seed into a female clam,
as the egg births into the mother,
as seven months pass,
then hatched children.
Adoring them we do,
devoting ourselves,
teaching them, making self-sacrifices
for food, clothing, shelter
and toys they need.
To our elders
that teach us.
Praying, doing good deeds,
whom we lavish in the after life,
with more riches than any world
could offer.

So precious diamonds of wonders to feel
the skies,
precious gems of every sort,
a Narnia, a neverland world.
Of the unthinkable imagination,
of all great
fantasies and dreams made by
the rich creator.

Swatter

Pesky bugs who bother me,
will receive their death spell from
the dreadful fly swatter I hold.
Having been hit, it splatters
its guts, crushed, it's a yucky spew,
dried then dead,
as bothersome insects wither way.
No more pest but doomed to
its death, by my bug swatter.

Egg Man

The chicken has gone on her rounds,
Leaving her little eggs exposed. As the
farmer creeps inside the hen house
contemplating a stealth move for snatching the
eggs. As the rooster crows singing his morning
hymns, as humans grow hungry,
eggs snatched then to the farmer's house,
runs the egg man from the rooster.
Soon to be cracked, fried and relished
by humans
wanting their breakfast.

The Pig

Gobbling mouthfuls of sausage, honey-baked ham, and bacon,
snacking on Babe Ruth or Snickers candy bars,
devouring wholesome chocolate mousse desserts,
for breakfast, lunch and dinner,
such is the life of the hog-man.
Lemon-meringue and cherry pies are his lovers,
brewed beer he drinks like water,
and sugar he eats by the kilogram,
ingesting food by the pounds,
he grows large, looking more like a whale
consuming all lard,
to form his round, pudgy bottom,
and an Alaskan bear's belly,
always hungry and longing for bee's honey.
He's constantly gobbling, devouring everything
from Mother Earth's pudgy cheeks–
such is the oblivious swine.

Violin

Deep in the hills of the Vermont forest,
trapped in the dense grained wood of a maple tree,
lies a soul
longing to be heard inside the majestic halls of Carnegie.
Patiently it dreams of being spotted
by a master woodworker craftsman
who will, gently and masterfully,
hand carve from its wooden body
an angelic instrument known as the Stradivarius.
Ensconced it will lie protected
by a sturdy leather-covered case on the floor of
an aristocratic attic
where a young soul will unknowingly,
the iron latches unsnap,
to admire the light reflecting
from the shiny surface of
its curvaceous body.
Over the centuries,
many hands will with its strings fiddle
in a vain attempt to release the soul trapped within,
until one day, a virtuoso will,
with a few swift masterful strokes of taut horsehair,
unleash the untamed soul from its wooden lair
to showcase a crafty rhyming rhythmist,
of two souls dancing as one,
fiddling away until the day
he meets his grave,
awaiting his pass to the promised land,
where angels sing his melodic praise
of the master violinist that he be.

Clock

Clocks go moving fast yet slow
ticking seconds pass so many minutes at
hands
hours
go by, oh time flies, bells ring
at midnight, so many years
to tinker with, so we get born
oh days fly by. Near the last days
of our clock
moving fast in a
sand glass, then suddenly
out of sand.
Breathing are last breaths, in a hospital bed seeing the light
heading for the sky,
with no more life.
Clocks and tickers stop, no more
watches
but a dead clock
out of minutes. No more
batteries needed.
Sinking into the ground, in a coffin
for sure humanity has died, no more time left,
ceasing to exist. Then
comes our judgment
so we are judged.

Colors

Black or white, brown, red, or yellow,
we are all colors on a color wheel,
banded together we are
a rainbow in the sky,
accepting all adjacent colors,
so we blend in the color wheel
of life.
Humans co-existing with nature
in an ever evolving world
shaped by the hands of a majestic painter,
whose crayons,
the size of a storm, a hurricane, or typhoon,
constantly paint a new picture of the world we inhabit.
The capricious moon,
sometimes white, other times cheesy yellow,
and sometimes dark like the night which surrounds it
forever playing with its celestial playmates,
in a giant playground extending beyond
the darkness of the night,
well into the light of day,
amusing the tiny multi-colored toy peasants that we be.

Bees in Love

Honey, my sweet lover bee,
let these be the days,
of bees in love,
flowers for the queen,
kisses for the king,
choirs singing
church bells ringing
offer thee my ring,
wedding is to be,
let me hold your wing.

Human Dreams and Tails

Looking through the pupil of mother's
and father's eye at
a blue clear sky of sunshine days,
at a kite nearly kissing the sun,
a cradled infant looks upon its new world
awed, amazed, and bewildered.

In short time,
mindful of the cosmic road of dreams of glory,
power and greatness,
he begins leaping, advancing, hopping,
from one job to another.

In a giant, spinning, spherical rat cage,
hands outstretched yet never touching the sun,
you're only saving up to pay for rent,
and then it's due again–
steadfast cycle has no tail,
and in an inevitable blink,
your last spin.

Twinkle, twinkle little eyes,
blowing bubbles towards the sky,
debuting your first tears and cries,
consuming your measured time on earth–
mine near its last phases,
yours only at genesis.

Timeless Hearts

It was a cloudy, cold winter day
as I felt the morning breeze sweep
past my body.
I saw the heavy clouds
release their gift of snowflakes
over the frozen snowman
as leaves fell to the ground
leaving barren tree groves shivering
in their roots.
I knew it was winter's turn to showcase
her beauty, as the yawning sun
slowly emerged, to melt the snow.
The sad snowman cried
while my rosy cheeks
thawed out, I sighed the happiness
of cold hearts. My family,
dressed as white snow leopards,
sled past the downward sloping
hill, while my brother and I
dashed through the snow
happier than deer prancing
gleefully
I felt transported to a
mystical realm called the Golden Era where
only true happiness and love existed.
Treasures were
all around us.
But those were only fond memories now.
Ten snowy seasons had elapsed to strip the trees
and ten leafy dresses mother nature to them lent.

But where was my family now?
Taken away by the snow devil?
I felt so sad. No more snow fights
or sled rides.
I miss the image of mother's sky-blue eyes and
father's tugging of my sled rope.
Only distant faint memories now.
Gone were the days when we made snow angels
in the frost and gave each other cheek Eskimo kisses.
How the family all adored those treasured
moments of internal love which were to last
forever.
Remember the great snow fights we had, and
the unstoppable fun? So many games and jokes,
those joyous moments, only two
brothers could have.
Why had God, or time itself taken them away?
Only the memories remained, and those too
would in time fade.
The only relic left was a gold-plated Peter Pan coin in
my brother's corduroy pants.
Everyone was moving on,
becoming adults, except me, forever young.
My only hope now was to awaken in the heavens
to see my family walking gently over a gray
misty rain-laden cloud.
I was on top of the world, looking down,
watching those wonder years being relived
perpetually in slow motion.
Like a sparkle in the dark cosmos, our best
days eternally conjoined our timeless hearts.

Julie

Oh Julie, how I loved to behold your striking beauty,
the glow in your eyes, your girlish smile, and the yellow silky
spaghetti-hair which I could seemingly eat with tomato sauce.

Your girlish smile shooting arrows atop a
black, trampling, stallion,
those childhood memories would never fade.

The humble family shire you left,
my sole comfort you became,
the willow cloud to her prince.
Two summers gone,
your ripe honeydew melon I had become,
our love glistened in the sun.

A lovely darling princess you were back then,
on our wedding that winter day,
and soon another Christmas came.

A joyful present you were to me, year after year,
an ornament in the sky,
hanging in that heavenly Christmas tree.
A seed was planted in you.
A creation brought forth – more morning stars to behold
in the heavens.

My bride a queen and I her king,
until the day our love shattered,
like an hourglass pouring
out our sand.

Our love turned to hell,
no kisses, no hugs, just
hot steamy lava,
only cries, pains, and screams
in a fiery lake.
No longer a precious diamond always
shining in the sky, my Julie.
Lost many years ago,
in the dark clouds of jealousy
and supposed infidelity.
Gone were the crown years
of castles in the high-arching sky
when I lost sight of you.
Only a ghost you became, lost in the castle
of darkness, in a maze of hazes–
a labyrinth of witches casting their spell and serving
a prince of darkness.
Oh what have you become? Are you lost in a trance?
Your heart, broken into pieces,
in need of an enchanted prince.
The truth, a beam of light,
to sooth and mend,
convinced you of the charming
faithful prince I was.
Now two hearts conjoined,
shone light and new life, with an enchanting kiss.
Suddenly you awoke – breaking the spell.
"Thank you my dear King. Faithful and true, forever mine."
An entranced Julie smiled.

Golden Jesus

Golden child descending,
arriving to your humble abode, your earth,
so long we've been waiting
to learn your teachings
to learn about your faith.
Oh Jesus,
we have been waiting for your arrival.
Oh graces sing
your love tonight, for we learn the golden rules.
Seeing the angels on the rise.
Tonight Christ bleeds less
learn to not sin.
Let's turn
the tide between the darkness and light.
Oh morning star gilt, one gift wishing to rise
for the golden one be the chosen sun.
The likes of God's might,
let's turn the tide from
hate to love, oh sinners we cry, for Christ.
Then comes rain,
when good things happen
a rainbow on the other side then comes, at the
end a leprechaun prize.
Golden Jesus we forge,
make us wealth, like that we treasure.
Oh good Lord we are humble for
we do your labor of the savior
and prophet Raven Joe
for evermore.

Desert Snowman

The cold white Seattle winter snow
in the palm of my hand,
glints the purities of life,
the happiness of winter times,
just as the black Saudi oil glints
the richness and joy of summer beach Arab sand.
Two earthly riches, kept a half-world apart
never living on the same land.
If only one could trade
the white gold in my palm
for a quart of dark oil from Arab soil.
Your oil, my snow –
each a different colored gem
in the other's eyes.
White gold, black gold,
we share our wealth
trading our fortunes
exclaimed the dreary desert snowman
to the lost and lonely forest dune man.

Carnage

The night was eerily quiet and my mind
drifted towards the lessons learned in the aftermath
of the war. The turmoil had ruined our fertile lands
and I thought about the tranquil life I had lost herding
cattle, farming cotton, and living on the family farm.
I caught a fleeting image of the beautiful Southern women
at a dance hall in their exquisitely manicured mansions.

The current hostilities had altered my course of life.
Next to me, lying in a pool of blood lay my
good buddy Jimmy, atop the
grassy knoll. His stomach lay torn to flesh as his
intestines wound like a hose on the ground and
blood poured red gory ooze.
The ground meat of other dismayed infantrymen
lay astray on that gruesome slaughter field.

Those were images I could not forget. Flies were everywhere
feasting on the decomposed mucus of
other soldiers dying in agony among the many corpses in
the battle for the fields of Gettysburg.

Poor Jimmy. I covered him with a blanket and I
withdrew bandages from my medical kit.
I could not save Jimmy.
His last words were "freedom, long live the South"
and "Mary Lou". He was a brave heart. Nothing could
diminish his pride. He was the best soldier and
would surely be awarded
a medal for valor. But why did he have to die?

Would I be next? My eyes boiled with anger.
I could hear the
thumps on the ground as cannonball artillery fell,
creating small earthquakes that rippled through the campfire.
Then, like a piercing dart arrow, I was hit.
The enemy had gotten me.

My confederate legion fell that night.
What a day to die on one's birthday.
My eyesight faded and I felt numb.
Everything appeared either white or invisible.
Ghosts could be seen stepping over dead bodies.
I awoke in a stretcher after what seemed to me to be
hours and days melted into one.
My eyes could once again see the
vivid colors all around me.
My wife lay next to me. We were conjoined.
She placed two I.D. tags on my chest. One was
Jimmy's. The other mine.
"Long live General Lee and the Confederacy,"
she whispered in my ear.

Brewery

Dearest friend of mine,
Oh how I love thy bitter taste
and sight of bubbling beer foam.
I indulge in thee and
grab a frozen Bavarian beer mug.
One shot after another,
I quench my indomitable thirst,
just loving the high life,
no worries here, my shames all forgotten,
while my beer belly
burps and
gargles consuming
first-rate draft beer.
I am feeling quite drunk and
smell like your average
skunk.
That irresistible
brew of malt ale I long for,
since it be my dear friend.
Every night at the saloon, you'll find me
gobbling down
this elixir, for I be an alcoholic–
a drunk who sees no other love but
in his beloved beer mug.

Flower

From tiny seed to full adolescent bloom,
all dressed-up in a multi-petaled dress to adorn her stem
she is nature's eyes–
a reflection of
and witness to the
affection and love of a very first date,
lovely, hopeful smiles reflected on faces of bride and groom,
undying hope and healing at the end of a hospital bed,
comfort to the saddened hearts
who remember their dearest ones at a funeral,
and faith as she reappears shining amongst the grass
near a tombstone,
completing her cycle, blossoming,
gleaming happiness for eternity.

Glory Days

Dear brother Robert,
I miss those times when we were young,
when we had a glimpse of the stars' glint
and the heavens where we hoped
to live someday. Do you remember gazing
at the Andromeda Galaxy through our own
telescope? We were destined to go there,
two young space cadets venturing forth across
Ganymede and the other moons of Jupiter.
Remember those autumn days when we
were lost in the forest trying to find
the mythical Sasquatch we called Chewbacca?
One winter night it was so cold we nearly froze
into our Han Solo and Luke Skywalker action figures.
We warmed ourselves with log scraps
using a hand saw as if though it was a light saber cutting
into the belly of a Tauntaun reptomammal
from the rebel moon Hoth, like in the movie,
The Empire Strikes Back.
We pretended to be stranded on the rebel moon Hoth.
We were lost in the woods and were growing hungry.
The thought of killing an innocent deer
was disturbing us.
How could we
kill an innocent animal, a creature of Earth?
Oh grandfather I miss those days fishing with
the "old man of the sea" and with my brother who fell
into the riverbed trying to fish for salmon.
Oh how we envisioned the sea with mermaids
as we swam through the lakes.

Glory be to the times we had hiking up the trails
in Yosemite National Park in California,
while singing that song "Aint no mountain
high enough."
Looking back, at the retro eighties,
I can still see us playing centipede
games at the arcades and humming along to
the many one-hit wonders that we jammed to.
And then one day you vanished.
You went away to college and lived on your own.
You made new friends and girlfriends.
So many summers you were gone.
Skywalker adventures for us, no more.
Last summer, your lovely wife, you introduced.
We all loved
and during Thanksgiving,
a grandiose feast of father's favorite barbecue
chicken and mama's best tasting pumpkin pie we enjoyed.
Your presence brought back
many wonderful memories.
Now nothing could ever divide us. The force
was with us again.
Very truly yours,
your brother Steve.

Madness

Your reflection, I can see, in those empty haunted eyes,
in that deep stoic stare,
and awfully awkward
smirk staring back at me through this mirror.

What are you?
An horrific monster – a Dr.
Jekyll, Mr. Hyde – a twisted, conflicted, bent soul
who loathes in self-pity and despair.

Let me be. Move along – vacate my mind.
Like a shadow, you stalk me,
but I feel trapped in Van Gogh's scream,
confused and angry I now be,
for the evil which I have become.
I toil for the devil's bidding, for my actions he dictates.
I'm gone in search of my master to appease.

Oh devilish sinful deeds I do,
like sorcery, blasphemy, theft, lies,
and cheating others.
For my neighbors, no respect I now show
but instead
I laugh at their innocent faces.
Behind a mask of deceit
and subtle craftiness I hide, while they
unsuspecting of my snake-like mind,
more in me entrust.

I know not about performing
good deeds or about compassion, kindness,
or love.
Only for myself I think of–
a fiend of knights to say the least.

No happiness or peace is found wherever I turn
but plight and turmoil.
To find an arch-enemy of
saints I strive. Oh madness
entangled in your web, a creep I have become.
What have you done to me?
Interminably, inconsolably I weep.

Vessel

Birthed we are as a tiny seed
like a fish, that swims to find
comfort in a willing egg
that grows daily with the
gentle motherly caresses of a loving hand
over a nourishing womb as
she slowly weaves the yarn-like genes
in her tummy loom for months – just nine.
She bears an infant,
its nose identical to hers, and hair just the same,
all coded in fresh genes,
passed on from generation to generation
over the span of time.
With the same hand that rocks the cradle,
she holds up the infant in her fragile hands,
as a bewildered mind processes the world
bequeathed to him by his predecessors.
The child grows,
with passing time,
no longer needs the breast that feeds it.
Its first words now learns,
its own journey begins,
each eager unmeasured step
a new adventure, exploring his world
testing its boundaries.

Many life lessons soon will follow,
in a school where dreams are dreamt,
reality is masked,
and only time'll unveil
the unimagined harsh realities
survival will entail.
Great full years arrive,
morals and values slowly shape,
while school teachers
its global outlook help create,
and maidens its sensual desires help to tame.
What has from this ordeal been learned?
Is to the next generation
passing on what we have learned
to the young who one day grow old
dying then going from one place to another
cradled by the universe,
like a vessel that travels a starship,
from stars that burning hellishly
so we burst like fire, or good moral we become like
light in the maker of clouds,
to the world that breathe other earths, the offspring becoming
a part of us. Birthed again as a creation of many
in the mighty universe and
dreamful
realms
in the king's land
that molds us.

Hood Life

I'm going downtown, to watch the fights,
down in the hood, where boys be robbing,
from pockets and purses,
a place full of dangers,
a gang member haven,
small-time bandits doing the bidding for the rich
who lavish in wealth driving luxurious cars,
living in mansion penthouses.
Back in the boy's hood
jackknives be springing,
boys be stealing from banks and markets
with assault guns they
rant and rave,
of sending someone to a fiery grave.
They be taking beers and ecstasy to make a girl mate
or if not,
chained to a bed, enslaved.
What a war down
in the slums, what a menace in the ghettos, a hideaway and
drug zone of smokes and dopes.
Oh Christ, here comes the man with the badge,
followed by the one with the cross.
For they will bring justice and peace to the good old hood.